SEEDS

AND MORE SEEDS

SEEDS
AND MORE SEEDS

by Millicent E. Selsam

pictures by Tomi Ungerer

HARPER & ROW, PUBLISHERS
NEW YORK, EVANSTON, AND LONDON

A Science I CAN READ Book

To

EZRA

(the original seed-happy boy)

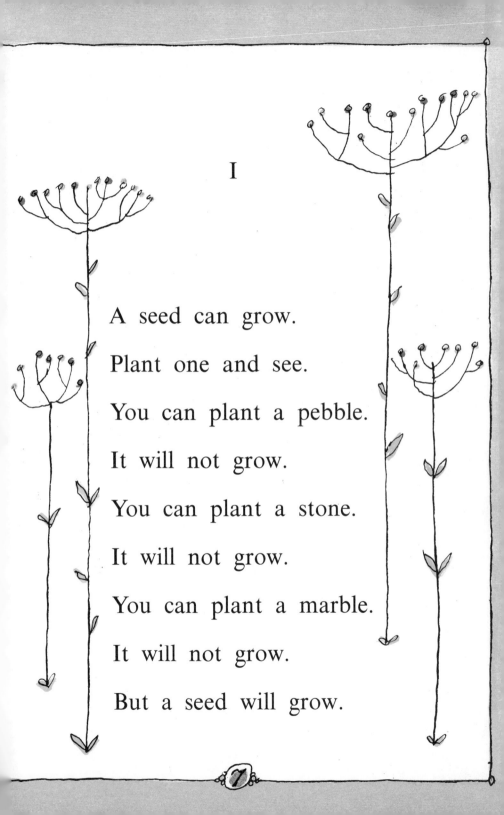

I

A seed can grow.

Plant one and see.

You can plant a pebble.

It will not grow.

You can plant a stone.

It will not grow.

You can plant a marble.

It will not grow.

But a seed will grow.

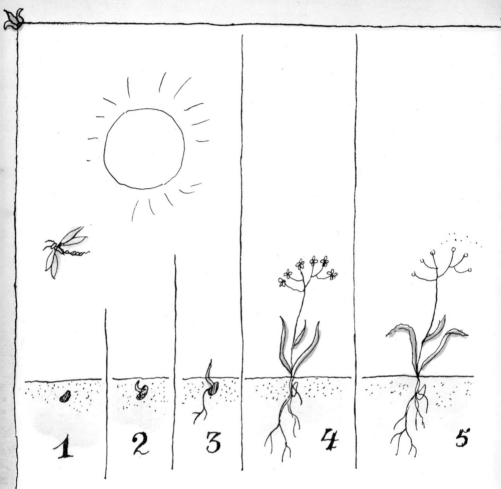

A seed is wonderful. It grows.

Something comes out of the ground.

A green stem comes out.

Little leaves get bigger.

A new plant comes out of the seed.

Here is Benny.

Benny wanted to know.

Can a stone grow?

Can a pebble grow?

"Plant them and see," said his father.

"Plant them in these pots.

If a stone can grow,

if a pebble can grow,

you will know."

Benny planted his stone in one pot.

He planted his pebble in another pot.

"I will put water in them.

If stones and pebbles can grow,"

said Benny,

"they will grow in these pots."

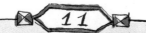

Benny found something else.

"Can a marble grow?" he said.

He planted it in another pot.

"If I water it

I will find out

if a marble can grow."

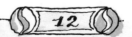

Then Benny found a shiny round thing.

"That is a seed," said his father.

"Can a seed grow?" said Benny.

Benny took another pot.

He planted the seed.

He put water in the pot.

Benny had four pots now.

The one with the pebble,

the one with the stone,

the one with the marble,

and the one
with the shiny round seed.

Benny waited.

Then one day, a little green stem came up in one pot.

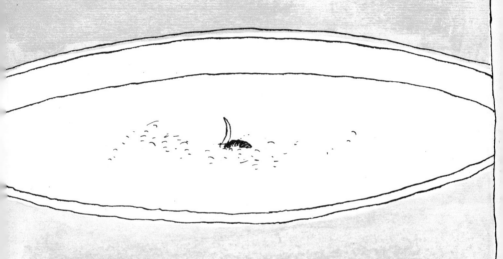

It did not come out of the pebble.

It did not come out of the stone.

It did not come out of the marble.

But it did come out of
the shiny round seed.

And then Benny knew

that a seed could grow.

Why does a seed grow?

Look inside a big seed to find out.

Find the baby plant

with tiny leaves

and the little part that becomes

the root and stem.

This baby plant

can grow into a big plant.

Benny wanted to know

why a seed grows.

He asked,

"Why is it that nothing will grow

from a pebble

from a stone

from a marble

but something

does grow from a seed?

What is in the seed?

What is in there that grows?"

"Open one and see," said his father.

And he gave him a big bean.

"A bean is a seed," he said.

"Open it and look inside."

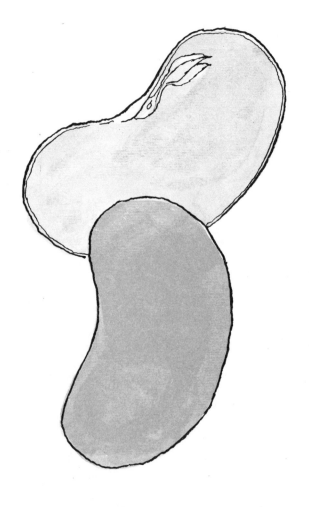

Benny opened the bean.

He found the baby plant inside.

"I will plant a bean," said Benny.

"I will water it.

Then the baby plant in the seed

will grow."

Benny planted a bean.

He watered it every day.

And the bean grew.

It grew and grew.

It got bigger and bigger.

It grew into a big bean plant.

"I want more seeds," said Benny.

"I will plant them in pots

and water them and make them grow."

First his father gave him
some more beans.

Benny planted red beans.

He planted white beans.

He planted black beans.

He planted brown beans.

He planted beans with spots.

The red beans grew.

The white beans grew.

The black beans grew.

The brown beans grew.

The beans with spots grew.

They grew and grew

and got bigger and bigger.

They grew into big bean plants.

"They all look like my first bean plant,"
said Benny.

"I want something new!"

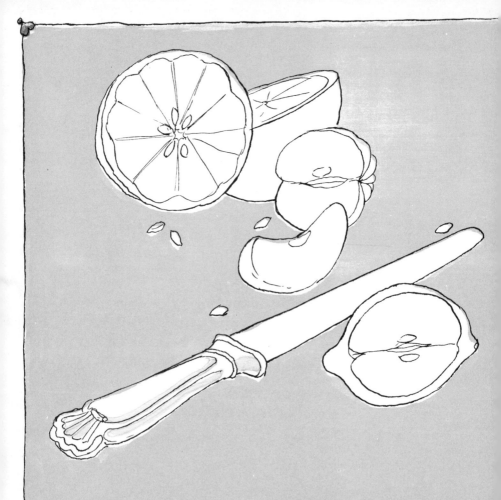

That day Benny's father gave him

the seeds of a grapefruit

the seeds of an orange

the seeds of a lemon.

Benny planted them.

He put the grapefruit seeds in one pot.

He put the orange seeds in another pot.

He put the lemon seeds in another pot.

He made a picture of a grapefruit.

He made a picture of an orange.

He made a picture of a lemon.

He put the pictures on the pots.

"Now when they grow," said Benny,

"I'll know which is which."

The lemon seeds grew.

The grapefruit seeds grew.

The orange seeds grew.

They all grew.

And all of them

had shiny dark green leaves.

"Without my pictures on the pots,"

said Benny,

"I would not be able

to tell them apart!"

"I want more seeds to grow,"
said Benny.

Then his father gave him
lentils from the lentil box
peas from the pea box.

And Benny grew lentil plants
and pea plants.

Then one day Benny

found some seeds himself.

He went to get food for his bird.

He saw the box.

He saw the word SEED.

He put some birdseed in his hand.

"These are seeds!" cried Benny.

"What will grow from these?"

He took a pot.

He planted the seeds.

Lots of plants came out of those seeds!

"My house was full of seeds,"

said Benny.

"And now it is full of plants!"

III

You can find seeds outside.

Go and look.

The wind blows them.

The water carries them.

The sticky ones stick to your coat.

Squirrels eat nut seeds and bury
some in the ground.
There are many kinds of seeds,
and every seed grows into the kind
of plant it came from.

After Benny planted every seed

he could find in the house

he said, "Where can I find more seeds?

I want more seeds to grow."

"Look outside, Benny," said his father.

"Look in the garden.

Look in the park.

Look in the street.

You will find seeds everywhere."

Benny went to look.

He walked around the garden once.

He walked around again.

Where were the seeds?

Then he stopped.

There in a little pile of mud

Benny found three seeds.

One was round and brown.

One was round and red.

One was round and white.

Benny took his seeds inside

and put them in a cup.

"I found some seeds,"

he called to his father.

His father came to look.

"You are a good seed hunter," he said.

"You found three seeds!

But here is a seed

that found you, Benny."

And there was a sticky seed

stuck to his coat.

"That makes four," said Benny.

Benny and his father

went to the park one day.

They saw a maple tree.

Up in the branches there were

bunches of seeds with thin green wings.

"Seeds!" said Benny.

"There are seeds all over that tree!

I want some."

"I cannot reach them," said his father.

Just then the wind shook the tree.

Benny ran to pick up the seeds

that sailed to the ground.

Benny and his father sat down.

A squirrel was digging a little hole.

It dropped a large brown seed inside

and covered up the hole.

"He is hiding an acorn,"

said Benny's father.

"If he does not find it later on,

it will grow into an oak tree."

"I'll make it grow into an oak tree,"

said Benny.

He dug up the acorn

and put it in his pocket.

On the way home,

Benny looked for more seeds.

He found some floating in a puddle.

He took them home too.

Benny planted the maple seed,

the acorn,

the seeds he found

in the garden in the mud,

the round brown one

the round red one

the round white one

the sticky seed that stuck to his coat

and the little seeds

that were floating

in the puddle.

"Father," he said,

"when you find a seed outside,

you never know what will come out of it.

It could become a great big tree,

or a tiny little grass plant,

or maybe even a daisy.

But I saw the maple seeds fall

from the maple tree,

so I know what they will be.

And this acorn will become an oak.

If I know the plant the seed came from,

I know what it will grow into."

IV

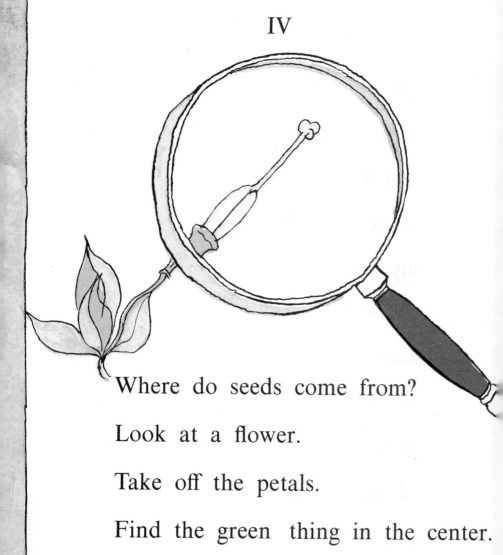

Where do seeds come from?

Look at a flower.

Take off the petals.

Find the green thing in the center.

It is called a pistil.

Down inside it seeds will grow.

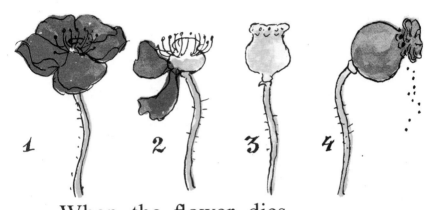

When the flower dies

and the petals fall,

the pistil gets bigger and bigger.

All the time, inside it, tiny little

seeds get bigger and bigger

until they are ripe.

Then they fall to the ground

and grow into new plants.

Benny found out where seeds come from.

One day he looked at his big bean plant.

He saw a flower.

He looked at it on Monday.

He looked at it on Tuesday.

He looked at it on Wednesday.

On Thursday,

the petals looked dry.

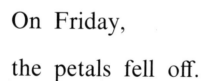

On Friday,

the petals fell off.

And that was when Benny saw the green thing in the center of the flower.

It looked like a little green boat.

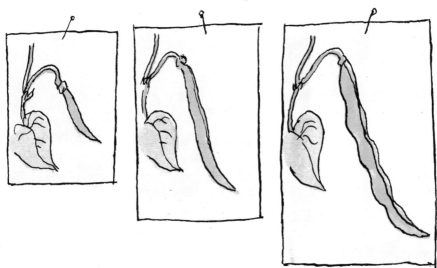

Benny looked at it every day.

It grew bigger and bigger.

Then he saw some bumps inside it.

As the green thing got bigger and bigger, the bumps inside got bigger and bigger.

Benny waited.

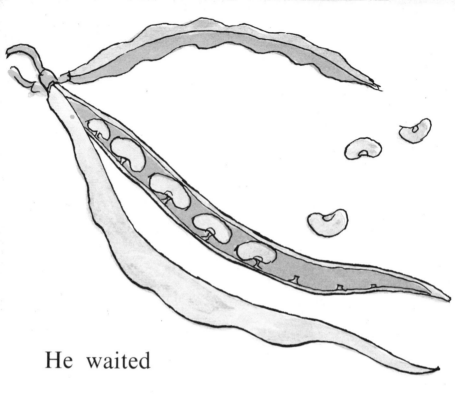

He waited

until the green thing was as big

as he thought it would ever get to be.

Then he picked it off the plant.

He split it open.

Those bumps were beans!

"These are bean seeds," cried Benny.

"I made my own seeds!

I made my own seeds!

Now I have more seeds to plant!"